UNDER MICHIGAN

To Allen Park Library —
Best Wishes! Thanks for
having me at "Meet the Authors"!
7/27/06

Great Lakes Books

A complete listing of the books in this series can be found online at http://wsupress.wayne.edu

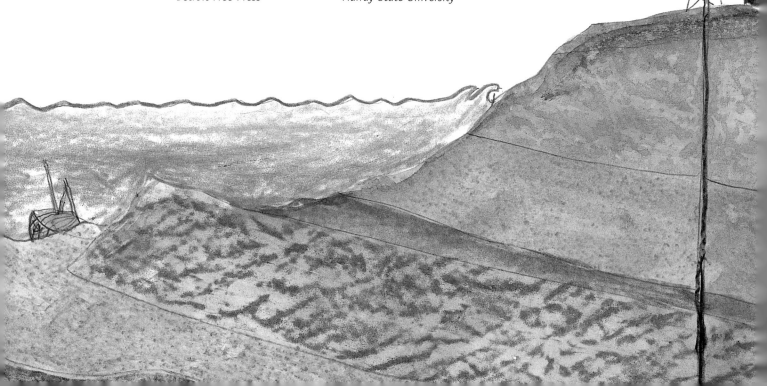

UNDER
MICHIGAN

The Story of Michigan's Rocks and Fossils

Written and Illustrated by Charles Ferguson Barker

Wayne State University Press
Detroit

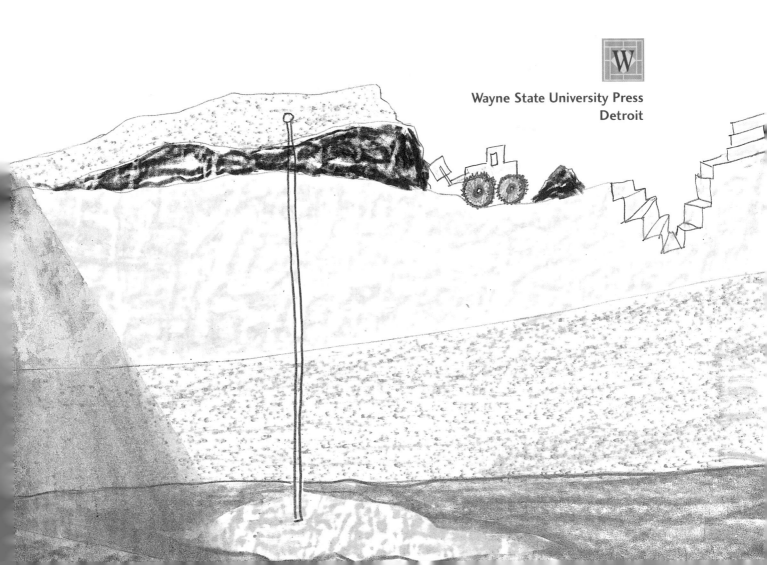

Manufactured in Canada.

09 08 07 06 05   5 4 3 2 1

Library of Congress Cataloging-in-Publication Data
Barker, Charles Ferguson.
  Under Michigan : the story of Michigan's rocks and fossils / written and illustrated by
Charles Ferguson Barker.
       p. cm. — (Great Lakes books)
  ISBN 0-8143-3088-6 (cloth : alk. paper)
 1. Geology—Michigan—Juvenile literature. 2. Geology, Stratigraphic—Juvenile literature.
I. Title. II. Series.
  QE125.B28 2005
  557.74—dc22
                                                              2004020808

Publication of this book was made possible through the generosity of the Friends of the
Great Lakes Books Series Fund.

To Kenny, Anne, and Charlotte

(in chronological order)

What's under Michigan?

Michigan is easy to find on a map of the United States because it is surrounded by the Great Lakes. From above, Michigan's Lower Peninsula looks like a mitten, and its Upper Peninsula (or U.P.) reaches out into Lake Superior, the world's largest freshwater lake. It's even easy to see Michigan from outer space.

Michigan's surface is covered with green forests and sparkling blue lakes. There are big, busy cities and small, quiet towns all over the state. We can all see what Michigan looks like from above, but have you ever wondered what's *under* Michigan?

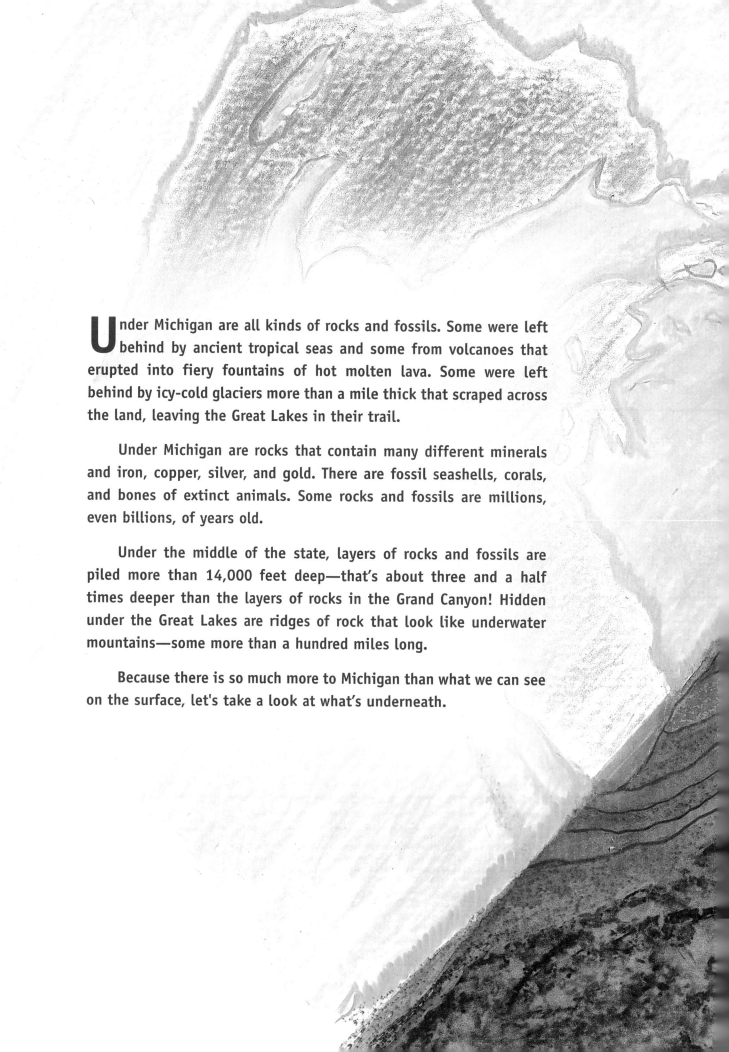

Under Michigan are all kinds of rocks and fossils. Some were left behind by ancient tropical seas and some from volcanoes that erupted into fiery fountains of hot molten lava. Some were left behind by icy-cold glaciers more than a mile thick that scraped across the land, leaving the Great Lakes in their trail.

Under Michigan are rocks that contain many different minerals and iron, copper, silver, and gold. There are fossil seashells, corals, and bones of extinct animals. Some rocks and fossils are millions, even billions, of years old.

Under the middle of the state, layers of rocks and fossils are piled more than 14,000 feet deep—that's about three and a half times deeper than the layers of rocks in the Grand Canyon! Hidden under the Great Lakes are ridges of rock that look like underwater mountains—some more than a hundred miles long.

Because there is so much more to Michigan than what we can see on the surface, let's take a look at what's underneath.

Michigan's Beginnings

The story of Michigan's rocks and fossils begins around 4.5 billion years ago when the earth was born—when there were only rocks, water, and air and before there were human beings, plants, and animals. The oldest rocks in Michigan are found in the U.P.

Geologists divide the earth's history into different time periods by classifying the age of rocks and fossils around the world. Just like we have names for months of the year and days of the week, we have names for these intervals of time since the formation of the earth. The geologic time interval we live in now—which started about 10,000 years ago—is called the Holocene epoch. Geologic time is so long that the periods are marked by major events in the earth's history, such as when plants or animals first appeared or when certain species became extinct.

The rocks and fossils under Michigan come from many different time periods, but rocks from some time intervals are missing. For example, rocks from most of the Mesozoic era—which ended when the dinosaurs became extinct, around 65 million years ago—are not found in Michigan. Water and wind may have swept them away, or perhaps the land was slowly rising and no layers of sediment were left behind, or deposited. Geologists sometimes call this time period the "lost interval." Without rocks or fossils to use as clues, scientists can only guess about what happened in the past.

One of the world's oldest known megascopic fossils—a fossil we are able to see without a microscope—was found in the U.P. It is about 2.1 billion years old.

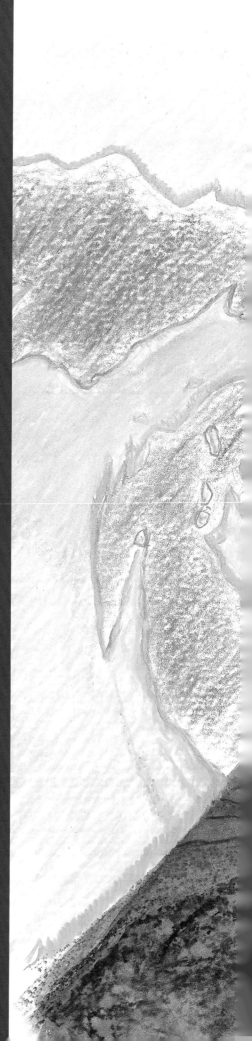

Major Time Period	Smaller Subdivision	Years Ago	What Was Happening
		Present time	Your birthday
CENOZOIC ERA	Quaternary		Time of most recent glaciations
		1,800,000	
	Tertiary		Humans show up
		65,000,000	Dinosaurs extinct by the end of this time period
MESOZOIC ERA (mostly missing in Michigan)	Cretaceous		
		145,000,000	
	Jurassic		First birds
		213,000,000	Many dinosaurs
	Triassic		First mammals
		248,000,000	
PALEOZOIC ERA	Permian		Major extinction of life in oceans (including trilobites)
		286,000,000	
	Pennsylvanian		First reptiles
		325,000,000	More swamps
	Mississippian		
		360,000,000	Many sharks Lots of swamps (later turned to coal)
	Devonian		Many shallow seas
		410,000,000	First land plants
	Silurian		Seas cover Michigan
		440,000,000	
	Ordovician		First fish appear
		505,000,000	Many life forms with shells and hard parts appear (these make good fossils)
	Cambrian		
		544,000,000	Trilobites
PRECAMBRIAN ERA	Proterozoic		Microscopic life (fossils found in U.P. were of this age) Bedrock in U.P.
		2,500,000,000	
	Archean		Continents, oceans, and atmosphere form
		3,800,000,000	
	Hadean		
		4,500,000,000	Earth is born

Michigan's Rock Types

Under Michigan, you can find all three main types of rock in the world: igneous, sedimentary, and metamorphic.

IGNEOUS: Igneous rocks are mostly found deep underground in the "basement" of the state. In fact, the deepest rocks are called "basement rocks." They were formed when molten magma cooled and crystallized. Igneous rocks either cool slowly beneath the ground or cool quickly if they shoot up onto the surface in a volcanic eruption. Most of the igneous rocks in the Lower Peninsula are hidden by thick layers of sedimentary rocks. In parts of the western U.P., though, we can see some igneous rocks at the surface from volcanoes that erupted about 800 million years ago.

SEDIMENTARY: Sedimentary rocks are formed when other rocks break up into sediment—small bits of sand, silt, and clay—and are cemented together to form new rock. The sediment is carried by streams, glaciers, or wind until it finally settles

down into water or onto land. The layers of sediment pile on top of each other like clothes on the floor of a messy room. Over time, the grains of sediment harden together. This cementing turns the loose particles into sedimentary rocks.

Sometimes, pieces of plants, bones, or animal shells settle into the sediment. They become part of the rock and turn into fossils. We can tell how old some of the layers of sedimentary rock are by the types of fossils we find inside them.

METAMORPHIC: The word *metamorphic* comes from *metamorphosis*, which means change. Metamorphic rocks are created when existing rocks buried deep underground are transformed by heat and pressure. For example, marble is a metamorphic rock created from heating and squeezing the sedimentary rock limestone. If you look closely at a polished marble floor, you can see that the rock looks like it was heated up and squashed.

Michigan on the Move

Even though we can't feel it, Michigan is slowly moving. Most of the thick layers of rocks and fossils under Michigan were formed when Michigan was covered by warm tropical seas. That's because millions of years ago, Michigan was closer to the equator, where it is hot all year long.

Why does Michigan move? The earth's crust is made up of huge slabs of rock called tectonic plates that fit together like pieces of a jigsaw puzzle. The plates shift slowly around the planet, with the continents riding on their backs. If you look at a globe, you can see that the coastlines of South America and Africa look like they could fit together like pieces of a jigsaw puzzle. That's because they did fit together once. About 150 million years ago they drifted away from each other and the Atlantic Ocean formed between them. North America and the other continents also drifted apart, taking Michigan along for the ride.

Some geologists think the continents will come together again in about 500 million years. If that happens, Michigan will probably be back near the equator. But not before many more long, cold Michigan winters.

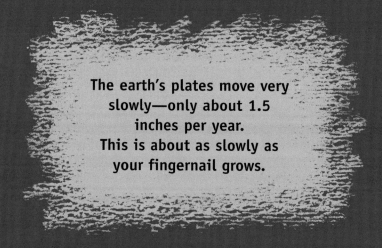

The earth's plates move very
slowly—only about 1.5
inches per year.
This is about as slowly as
your fingernail grows.

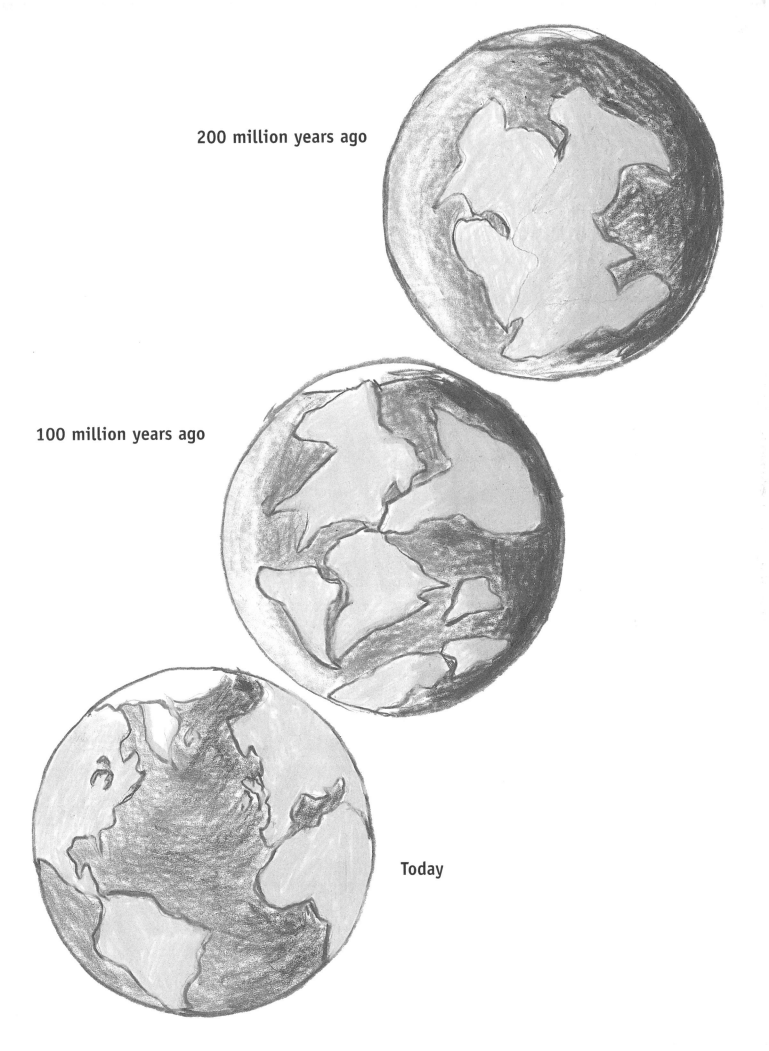

200 million years ago

100 million years ago

Today

Michigan's Tropical Seas

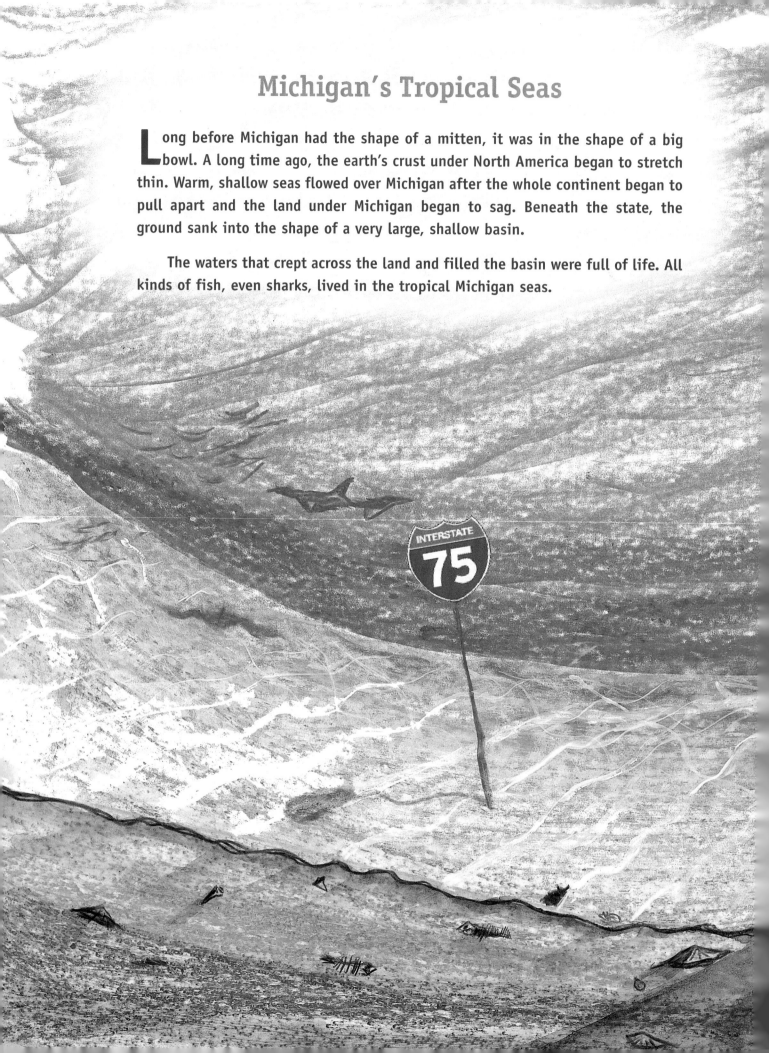

Long before Michigan had the shape of a mitten, it was in the shape of a big bowl. A long time ago, the earth's crust under North America began to stretch thin. Warm, shallow seas flowed over Michigan after the whole continent began to pull apart and the land under Michigan began to sag. Beneath the state, the ground sank into the shape of a very large, shallow basin.

The waters that crept across the land and filled the basin were full of life. All kinds of fish, even sharks, lived in the tropical Michigan seas.

The seas came in, dried up, and filled in again many times over hundreds of millions of years. Layer upon layer of sediment and fossils were deposited at the bottom of the seas. As the thick, heavy sediments from the oceans filled in Michigan's big bowl, the basin sank even deeper. Geologists all over the world call this area the Michigan Basin.

Downtown Devonian

Next Exit- 60 Million years

Rings of Rock

Over millions of years, layers of sediment settled on top of the layers beneath them, like smaller bowls stacked inside bigger bowls. Certain layers of sediment turned into very hard rocks that didn't get worn down as quickly as other, softer rocks next to them. Some of these harder rock layers "outcrop," or stick out from the surrounding land where we can see them, while others are hidden deep below the Great Lakes. One of these layers of hard rock is called the Niagara Group. It's from the Silurian age and is about 425 million years old.

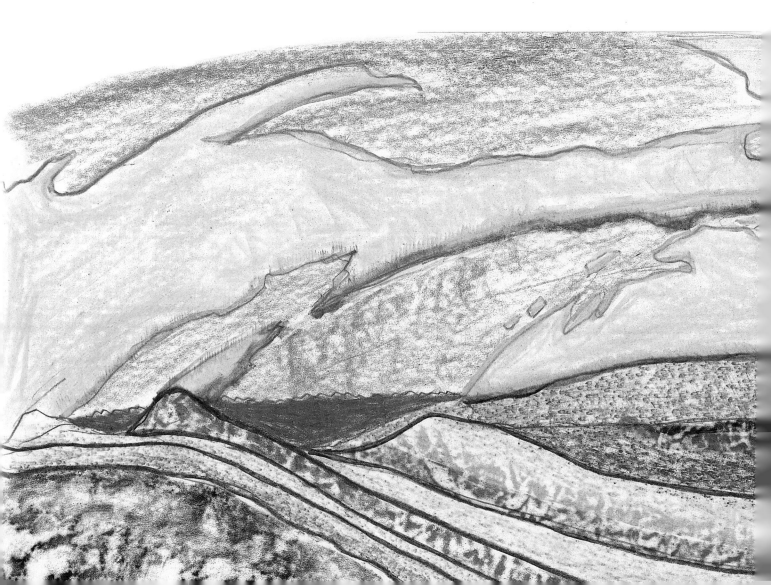

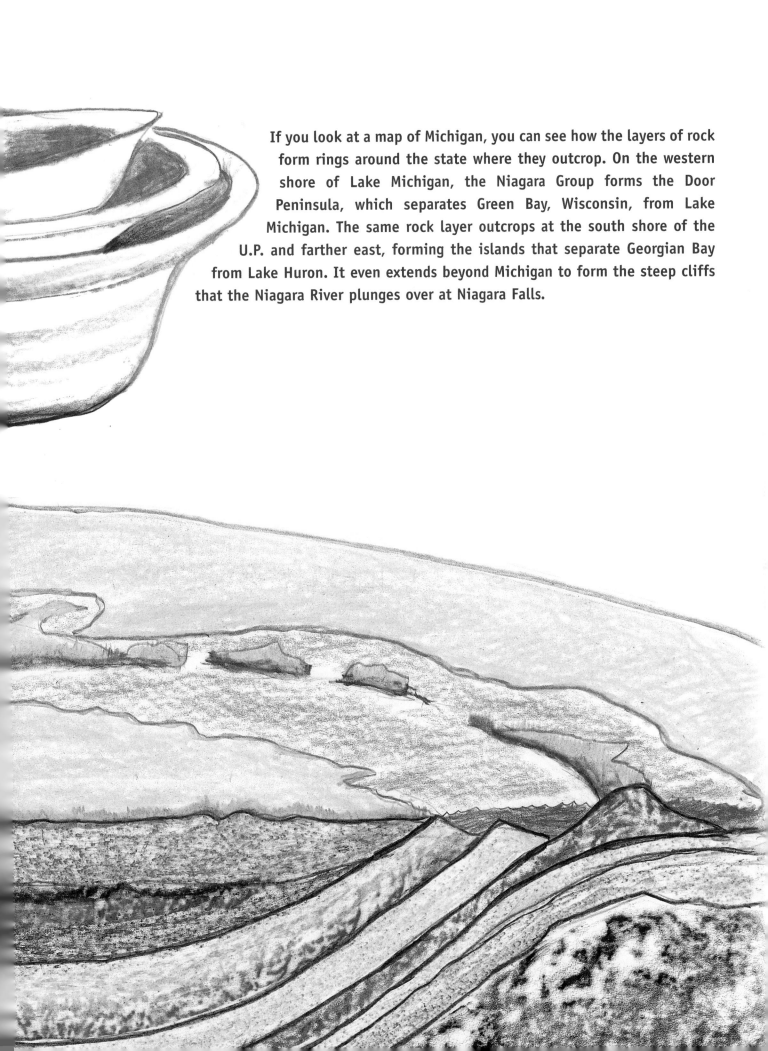

If you look at a map of Michigan, you can see how the layers of rock form rings around the state where they outcrop. On the western shore of Lake Michigan, the Niagara Group forms the Door Peninsula, which separates Green Bay, Wisconsin, from Lake Michigan. The same rock layer outcrops at the south shore of the U.P. and farther east, forming the islands that separate Georgian Bay from Lake Huron. It even extends beyond Michigan to form the steep cliffs that the Niagara River plunges over at Niagara Falls.

Michigan's Underwater Mountains

Under the Great Lakes are tall ridges and deep valleys with such names as the Chippewa Basin, Whitefish Fan, and the Alpena-Amberley Ridge. If we drained all the water from Lake Huron, ridges of rock higher than 400 feet in places and longer than 100 miles would tower over the lake floor.

Beneath the Great Lakes are huge underwater caves that formed when water dissolved holes in some of the softer rocks.

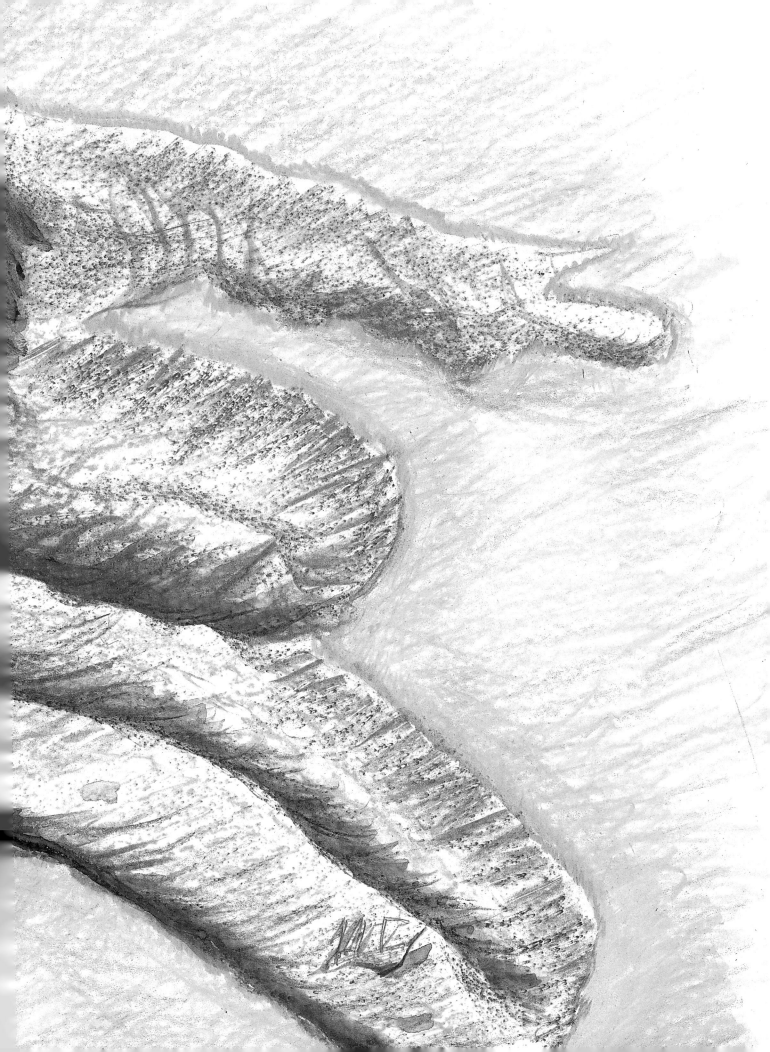

From Rocks to Resources

We can dig up different types of rocks, fossils, and materials deposited under Michigan and use them in many ways.

NATURAL GAS: Natural gas is formed when plant and animal remains are buried and decay. We can burn the gas as fuel for electrical power plants, stoves, and heaters. Some gas companies use Michigan's ancient buried coral reefs to store natural gas deep underground because the reefs have many tiny holes in them that can hold the gas. The reefs are surrounded by clay and other rocks that are sealed up tightly so the gas can't escape. Natural gas from as far away as the Gulf of Mexico and western Canada is piped into Michigan and pumped underground into the buried coral reefs. The gas is stored in the reefs during the summer when it isn't needed very much. In the winter it is pumped back to the surface where it can be used to heat our homes and schools, or piped to power plants to make electricity.

OIL: The oil found under Michigan comes from tiny organisms like algae that lived in the warm ancient seas. When the organisms died, they sank and piled up at the bottom of the sea. Over millions of years, sediment fell over the organisms until they were buried underground. Heat and pressure in the earth turned these organisms into oil. We use oil to make gasoline, plastic, and even ink for books.

COAL: The coal under Michigan formed from land plants that lived in Michigan's ancient swampy environment. When layers of sediment buried the swamps, the compressed plants slowly turned into dark, spongy peat. People often use peat in their gardens as a fertilizer to help plants grow. Plenty of peat can be

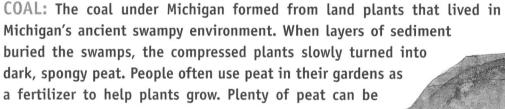

found around the "thumb" area of Michigan. After years of heat and pressure, the peat eventually turned into hard coal. Coal can then be used as fuel to make heat and electricity.

LIMESTONE: Limestone is sedimentary rock formed in the ocean and shallow seas. The soft mud of Michigan's tropical seas turned into rock after it dried and solidified, just like when wet cement hardens into concrete. Limestone is mined in several Michigan cities, including Alpena, Rodgers City, and Dundee. It is used to make cement for sidewalks, airports, roads, and buildings. Since limestone was once the bottom of a seabed, it can contain fossils. The next time you see a building made of gray or tan rock, look closely. If it's limestone, you may see some fossilized coral or shells.

METALS: The ancient rocks under Michigan's U.P. are rich in metals, including copper, iron, and—in a few places—silver and gold. These resources, even in small amounts, are very valuable, and they attracted early settlers to the U.P. Many mining towns were founded in "Copper Country" on the Keweenaw Peninsula.

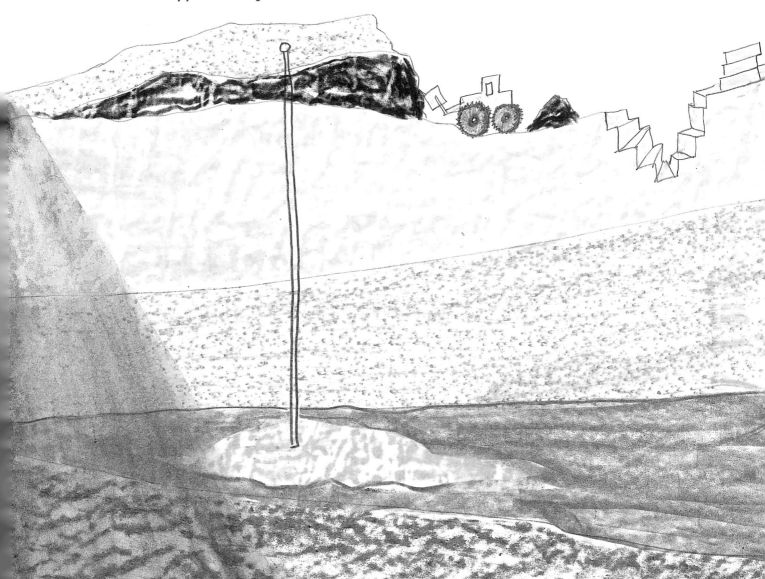

Michigan under Ice

In addition to the many rocks, fossils, and minerals left behind by tropical seas, there are rocks under Michigan left behind by thick icy glaciers.

About 2 million years ago—around the beginning of the Pleistocene era—the weather became colder and more and more snow began to fall. The snow couldn't melt during the short, cold summers, and over thousands of years it piled up and got tightly packed down into layers of solid ice. These layers became huge ice sheets, or glaciers. The ice sheets grew to a height of almost 2 miles and covered most of what is now Canada. The glaciers grew and slowly flowed to the south, down across Michigan and through the great river valleys that remained after the warm seas dried.

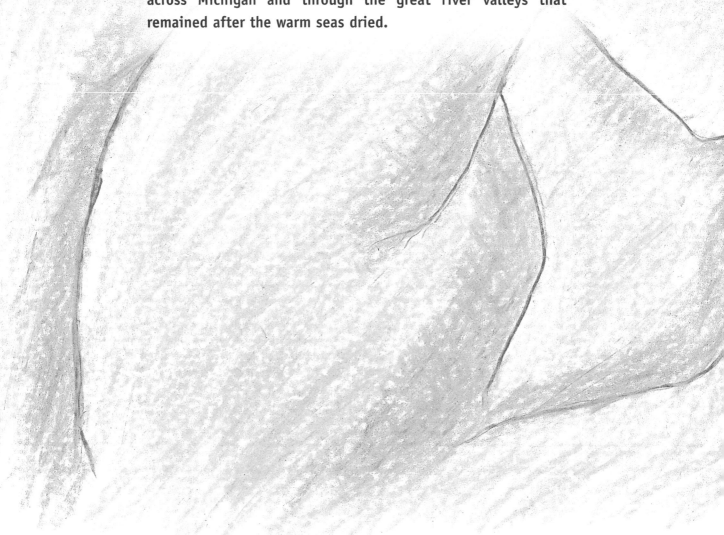

The river valleys were low places, making it easy for parts of the glaciers to creep into them. One section of a glacier, called a "lobe," moved up the valley that was where Lake Michigan is now, and another lobe moved up a valley that is now Lake Huron. Lobes of a glacier moved across the valleys that now make up Saginaw Bay and Lake Erie and spread across the land until most of the northern United States was under thick ice.

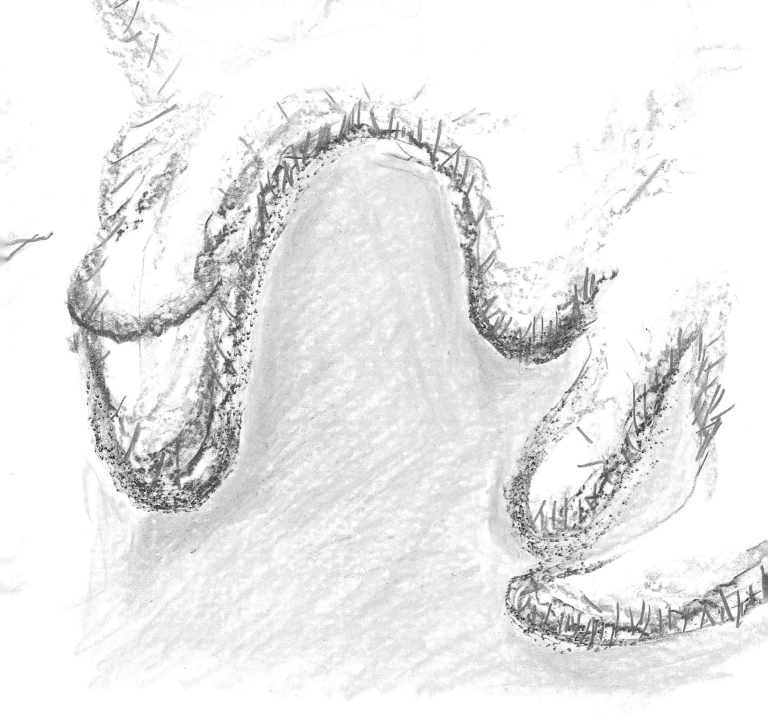

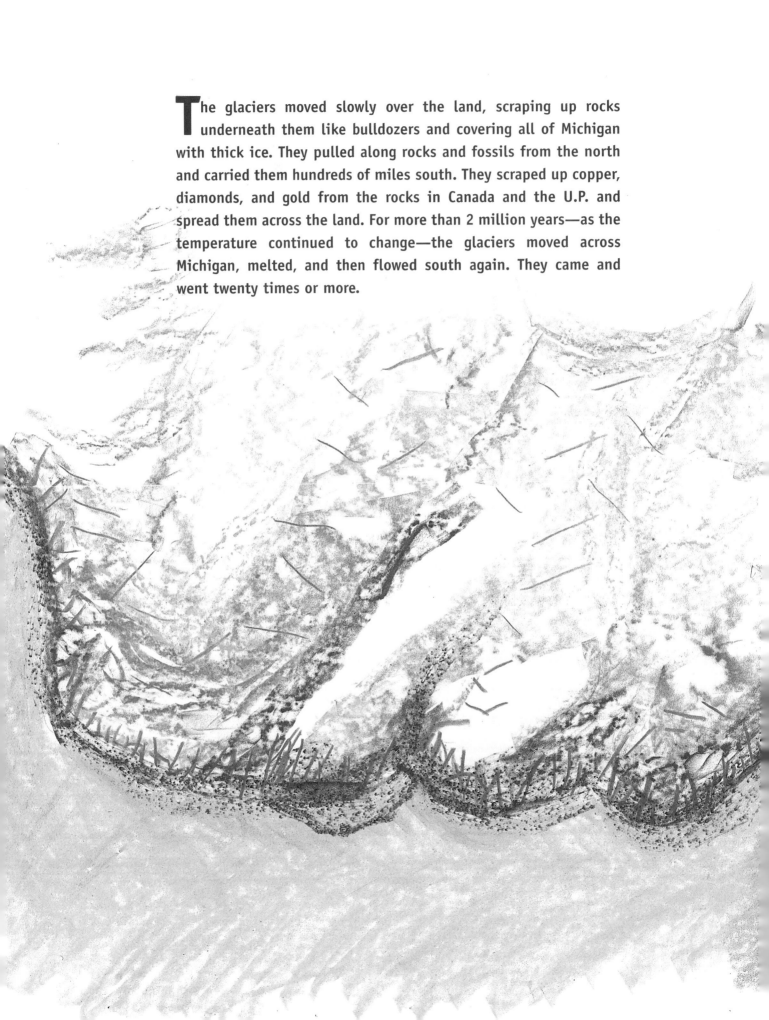

The glaciers moved slowly over the land, scraping up rocks underneath them like bulldozers and covering all of Michigan with thick ice. They pulled along rocks and fossils from the north and carried them hundreds of miles south. They scraped up copper, diamonds, and gold from the rocks in Canada and the U.P. and spread them across the land. For more than 2 million years—as the temperature continued to change—the glaciers moved across Michigan, melted, and then flowed south again. They came and went twenty times or more.

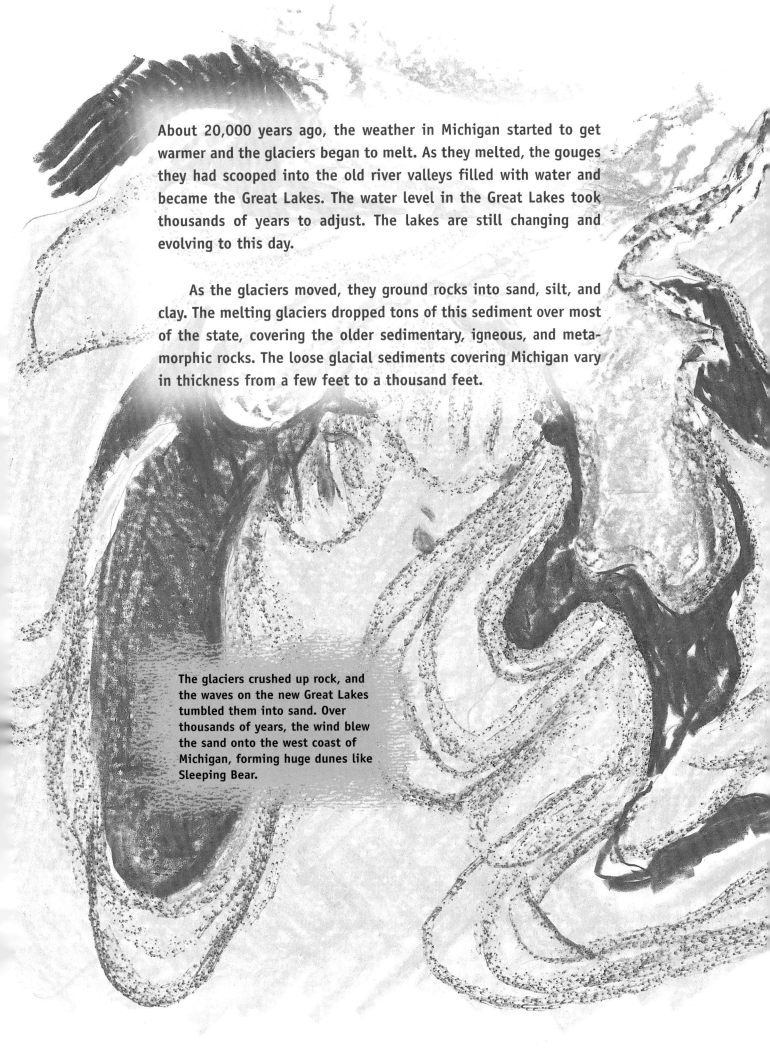

About 20,000 years ago, the weather in Michigan started to get warmer and the glaciers began to melt. As they melted, the gouges they had scooped into the old river valleys filled with water and became the Great Lakes. The water level in the Great Lakes took thousands of years to adjust. The lakes are still changing and evolving to this day.

As the glaciers moved, they ground rocks into sand, silt, and clay. The melting glaciers dropped tons of this sediment over most of the state, covering the older sedimentary, igneous, and metamorphic rocks. The loose glacial sediments covering Michigan vary in thickness from a few feet to a thousand feet.

The glaciers crushed up rock, and the waves on the new Great Lakes tumbled them into sand. Over thousands of years, the wind blew the sand onto the west coast of Michigan, forming huge dunes like Sleeping Bear.

The glaciers were so big and heavy that they actually pushed down the crust of the earth—just like when you press on the mattress of your bed as you lie down to go to sleep. About 10,000 years ago, after the glaciers finished melting, the weight of the ice was gone and the land slowly bounced back—just like when your mattress springs back up after you get out of bed.

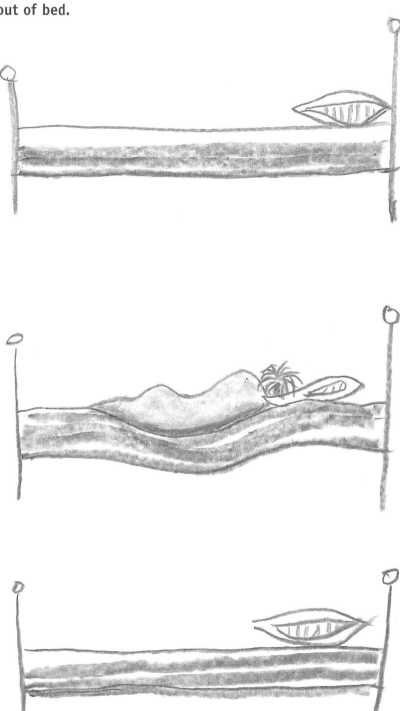

The weight of the glaciers pushed down the earth's crust the most where the ice was thickest. In northern Canada, near Hudson Bay, the crust was pushed down almost 1,000 feet and is still rebounding 10,000 years later. Northern Michigan is still rising in places—but very slowly, just two or three inches every hundred years.

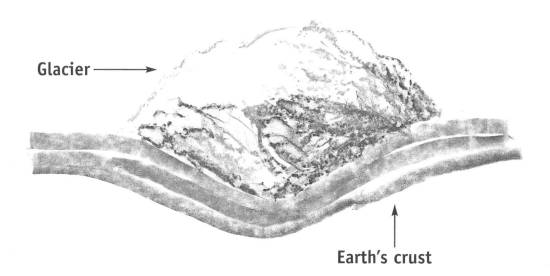

Glacier ⟶

Earth's crust ↑

Under Houghton and Munising are igneous rocks from volcanoes that erupted 800 million years ago. The city of Houghton and Houghton Lake are named after Michigan's first state geologist, Douglas Houghton. He mapped the geology of much of the state, particularly the copper and iron deposits of the U.P.

In the U.P. the rocks under Marquette, Escanaba, and Ishpeming are the oldest in the state at about 2.5 billion years old.

Under the surface of Kitch-iti-kipi, the "Big Spring" just west of Indian Lake in the U.P., you can see clear, clean water rushing out of the bedrock 45 feet below, creating underwater "volcanoes of sand."

In Traverse City, Harbor Springs, and Petoskey you can find fossilized coral from the seas that once covered Michigan 360 million years ago. These pieces of fossilized coral polished smooth by the waves are called Petoskey stones, and you can find them along the lakeshore. The Petoskey stone is Michigan's state stone.

Under Midland, Alma, and Owosso the sedimentary rocks are the thickest in the state at around 14,000 feet deep. In 1890 Herbert H. Dow pumped out seawater from a well drilled into these rocks and started the Midland Chemical Company. Using what he learned about making chemicals from Michigan groundwater, he founded the Dow Chemical Company.

Under the hills of Grand Rapids, Battle Creek, and Kalamazoo are thick deposits of rocks and fossils that were scraped up and dropped by glaciers.

Under Whitefish Point and along Pictured Rocks in the U.P., 500-million-year-old sandstones show us where ancient beaches used to be.

On Mackinac Island the rocks and fossils are 360 million years old. The island's famous Arch Rock was cut into Devonian Age limestone by waves when the lake level was about 100 feet higher than it is today.

Under Oscoda, only a few feet below the surface, an ancient whale bone was discovered. Thousands of years ago, whales from the Atlantic Ocean swam into the Great Lakes.

Rocks under Michigan

There are many different types of rocks, fossils, and minerals all over the state. Do you know what kinds are under or can be found where you live?

Under Flint are fossilized teeth from the sharks that swam in Michigan's shallow seas.

Under Lansing, all of the rocks of the Jurassic period are missing! They are part of the "lost interval" mentioned earlier.

Under Port Huron are rocks where oil was found for the first time in Michigan in 1886.

Under Ann Arbor and Saline are salt springs and Mastodon bones. The word saline means "salty," and both the town of Saline and its river were named for the salt deposits found there. The Mastodon, an extinct shaggy, elephant-like creature that roamed Michigan around 12,000 years ago, is Michigan's state fossil.

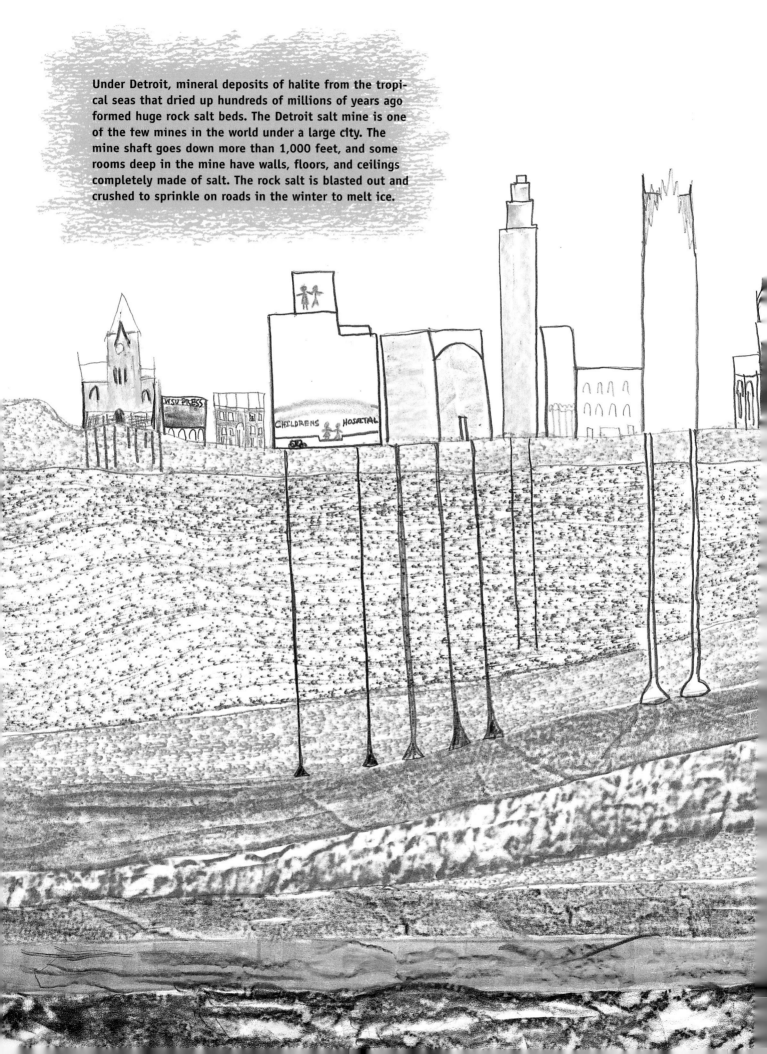

Under Detroit, mineral deposits of halite from the tropical seas that dried up hundreds of millions of years ago formed huge rock salt beds. The Detroit salt mine is one of the few mines in the world under a large city. The mine shaft goes down more than 1,000 feet, and some rooms deep in the mine have walls, floors, and ceilings completely made of salt. The rock salt is blasted out and crushed to sprinkle on roads in the winter to melt ice.

Under Michigan, there are rocks and fossils from tropical seas, rocks from hot volcanoes, and rocks left by glaciers that melted 10,000 years ago.

The story of the rocks and fossils of Michigan will never end. We don't know exactly when, but someday in the future Michigan will again be covered with thick, icy-cold glaciers and warm tropical seas.

If you look around, you will find many interesting rocks and fossils from all kinds of times and places. You'll probably find a fossil of a long-extinct creature from an ancient tropical sea . . . or maybe, just *maybe*, you'll find some diamonds or gold!

But best of all, you'll have fun just looking.

MICHIGAN GEOLOGICAL EXPLORATION

-FIELD NOTES-

Explorer_____

Date_____

Time_____

Location_____

Weather Conditions_____

Observations:

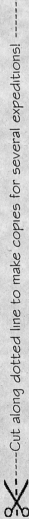

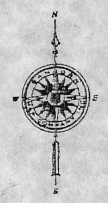

Inches

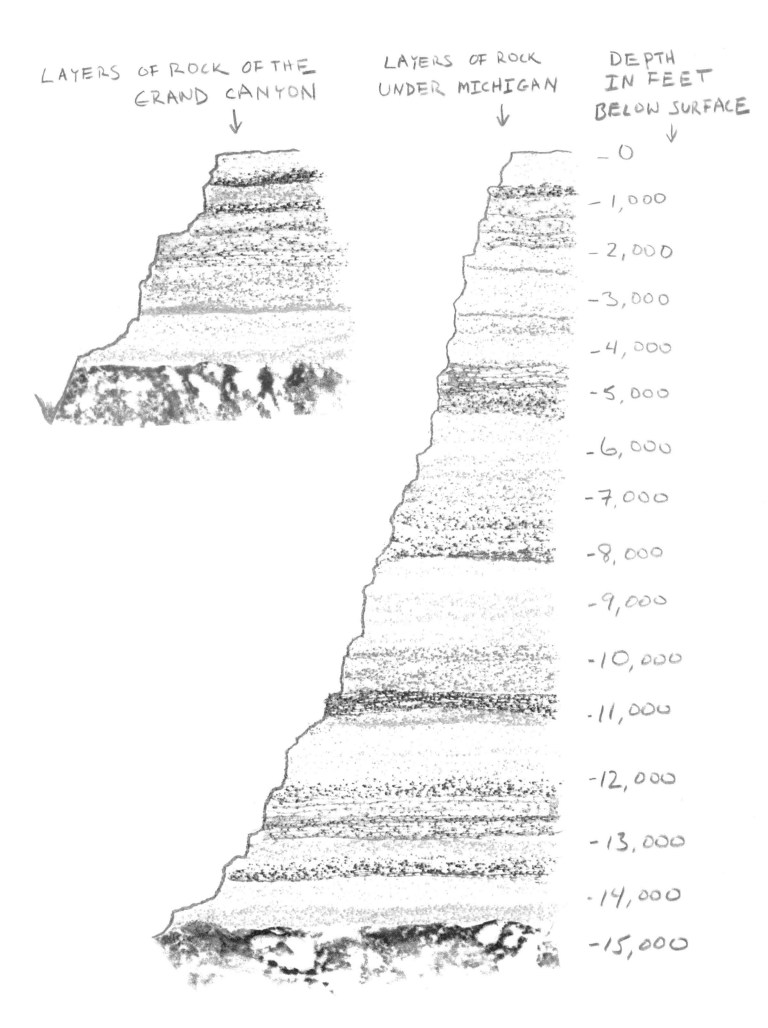

LAYERS OF ROCK OF THE GRAND CANYON ↓

LAYERS OF ROCK UNDER MICHIGAN ↓

DEPTH IN FEET BELOW SURFACE ↓

- 0
- 1,000
- 2,000
- 3,000
- 4,000
- 5,000
- 6,000
- 7,000
- 8,000
- 9,000
- 10,000
- 11,000
- 12,000
- 13,000
- 14,000
- 15,000

Glossary

Coal. Solid "fossil fuel" made up of ancient plants that lived in swamps, were buried by sediment, and were eventually compressed into a rock-like form.

Continent. Large landmass that rises above ocean basins (for example, North America).

Coral reef. Mound of often colorful and sharp growths on the ocean floor created by organisms that lived in shallow warm seas.

Crystallize. To turn to a solid form—such as minerals that form as molten rock cools.

Devonian. Geologic time period from about 410 to 360 million years ago.

Dinosaurs. Extinct reptiles that lived in the Mesozoic ("middle life") age. From the Greek words meaning "terrible lizard."

Extinct. When something has disappeared from the earth forever.

Fossil. Evidence of former life—parts of an animal, or its tracks—that eventually turned into rock (for example, an ancient shark's tooth, seashell, or dinosaur footprints).

Glacier. Huge mass of flowing ice that forms in cold climates where winter snow does not melt during the summer.

Holocene epoch. The current geologic time interval, which started about 10,000 years ago.

Igneous. Type of rock formed when molten magma or volcanic lava crystallizes.

Jurassic era. Geologic time period from about 213 to 145 million years ago.

Lobe. Smaller part or "arm" of a larger glacier.

Limestone. Sedimentary rock formed in ocean environments.

Megascopic. Large enough to be seen without a microscope.

Mesozoic. Geologic time period from about 248 to 65 million years ago.

Metamorphic. Type of rock formed from heating up and squashing other rocks.

Michigan Basin. The bowl-shaped geologic structure that describes the Great Lakes region.

Natural gas. Gas created from the decay of ancient organisms—a "fossil fuel."

Oil. Thick, dark liquid formed from ancient ocean organisms, such as algae, that were buried and transformed into a "fossil fuel."

Organism. Something living, or that was alive, such as a plant or animal.

Tectonic Plates. Huge slabs of rock that fit together like pieces of a jigsaw puzzle, forming the outer solid layer of the earth.

Sediment. Broken-up pieces of rock or organisms.

Sedimentary. Type of rock formed by sediment piling up, compressing, and cementing together.

Silurian era. Geologic time period from about 440 to 410 million years ago.

Tropical. Warm environment typical of areas near the equator (for example, Florida or Hawaii).

Volcano. Mountain or landform created when molten lava erupts onto the surface.

Places to Learn More about Michigan's Rocks and Fossils

Always call ahead to check the times that these exhibits and parks are open and to ask if there is an admission fee.

ALBION

Albion College, Department of Geology

611 East Porter St., Albion
517-629-0486 or 517-629-1000

Displays of minerals, rocks, fossils, maps, seismograph, and analytical lab.

Brueckner Museum of Starr Commonwealth

13725 26 Mile Rd., Albion
517-629-5591

Mineral and fossil exhibit.

ALMA

Alma College, Department of Geology

614 W. Superior St., Alma
989-463-7191 or 989-463-7198

The Alma college collection contains over 8,000 specimens of rocks, minerals, fossils and ores, a significant number of which are of museum quality.

ANN ARBOR

University of Michigan Exhibit Museum of Natural History

1109 Geddes Ave., Ann Arbor
734-764-0478
http://www.exhibits.lsa.umich.edu

Exhibits relating to fossils, minerals, geology, paleontology, and the natural sciences.

BATTLE CREEK

Kingman Museum of Natural History

175 Limit St., Battle Creek
269-965-5117

Natural history and science exhibits, including minerals and fossils.

BLOOMFIELD HILLS

Cranbrook Institute of Science

39221 Woodward Ave.,
P.O. Box 801, Bloomfield Hills
248-645-3200
http://www.cranbrook.edu

Fine mineral collection and outstanding display. Also exhibits on geology and fossils.

CALUMET
Keweenaw National Historical Park

25790 Red Jacket Road,
P.O. Box 471, Calumet
906-337-3168
http://www.nps.gov/kewe

This National Park comprises 16 different cooperating sites in the historic copper mining district. In addition to providing a wealth of information to tourists, the park maintains a large collection of photographs and archival documents available to researchers on request.

Coppertown U.S.A. Mining Museum

25815 Red Jacket Rd., Calumet
906-337-4354 or 906-337-4579

Exhibits on the history of copper mining in the Keweenaw, mining equipment, and specimens of native copper.

CASPIAN
Iron County Museum

P.O. Box 272, Caspian
906-265-2617 or (off season) 906-265-3942
http://www.ironcountymuseum.com

Historic buildings, exhibits, and dioramas featuring mining equipment and memorabilia, Caspian mine head frame, Lee LeBlanc wildlife art gallery.

CHELSEA
Gerald E. Eddy Discovery Center

Waterloo Recreation Area,
16345 McClure Rd., Chelsea
734-475-3170

Interpretive exhibits of rocks, minerals and fossils. Many hands-on geology displays as well as outdoor trails including the Rock Walkway. The Geologic Arts Fair is held in the fall.

COPPER HARBOR
Fort Wilkins State Park

P.O. Box 71, Copper Harbor
906-289-4215

Interpretive exhibits and programs depicting military and local lifestyles in the mid-1800's, including copper mining history; some minerals.

Astor House Museum

Minnetonka Resort, Highway 41,
Copper Harbor
906-289-4449

Mining memorabilia and Indian artifact collections, rocks and minerals, large antique doll collection, other collections.

DEARBORN
University of Michigan—Dearborn, Department of Natural Sciences

4901 Evergreen Rd., Dearborn
313-436-9129

Collection of minerals and fossils in the science building, including an extensive collection of geodes.

DELAWARE/MOHAWK
Delaware Copper Mine Tours

HC 1 Box 102, Mohawk
906-289-4688

Underground and surface mine tours.

EAGLE RIVER
Keweenaw County Courthouse

HC 1 Box 607, Eagle River
906-337-2229

Rock and mineral exhibit.

EAST LANSING

Michigan State University, Center for Integrated Studies and General Science

North Kedzie Lab Building, East Lansing
517-353-4572

Exhibits of rocks, minerals, and fossils. Also exhibits of minerals in Geology Department Library (in basement of Natural Sciences Building).

GRAND MARAIS

Gitche Gumee Agate and History Museum

E21739 Braziel St.,
P.O. Box 308, Grand Marais
906-494-2590

Lake Superior agates, local history memorabilia, and artifacts.

GRAND RAPIDS

Grand Rapids Public Museum

272 Pearl St. NW, Grand Rapids
616-456-3977

Interpretive exhibits of fossils, rocks, and minerals.

Michigan Natural Storage Mine

1200 Judd Ave. SW, Grand Rapids
616-241-1619

Old gypsum mine now used for cold and dry storage. Specimen collecting is permitted.

GREENLAND

Adventure Copper Mine and Campground

P.O. Box 6, 200 Adventure Rd., Greenland
906-883-3371

Underground mine tour.

HANCOCK

Quincy Mine Hoist

49750 U.S. 41, Hancock
906-482-3101

Surface and underground mine tours. Exhibits feature Nordberg steam hoist, mining history and equipment, minerals.

HILLSDALE

Hillsdale College Museum

Strosacker Science Center,
Hillsdale MI 49242
517-607-2607

Large collection of fossils, rocks, and minerals, as well as rotating public exhibits. Research collections are available by appointment only.

HOUGHTON

A. E. Seaman Mineral Museum

Michigan Technological University
1400 Townsend Dr., Houghton
906-487-2572
http://www.geo.mtu.edu/museum

Large collection and outstanding displays, especially of Michigan minerals. The Seaman Museum is the officially designated Mineralogical Museum for the State of Michigan, and offers the most comprehensive exhibits of both Michigan and worldwide minerals in the upper midwest U.S.A. The museum is located on the fifth floor of the Electrical Energy Resources Center building.

MTU Archives and Copper Country Historical Collections

Michigan Technological University
1400 Townsend Dr., Houghton
906-487-2505
http://www.lib.mtu.edu/jrvp/mtu-archives/mtuarchives.htm

Located on the third floor of the J. Robert Van Pelt Library, the archives houses one of the largest known collections of historic photographs and documents relating to Michigan's copper mining heritage.

IRON MOUNTAIN

Cornish Pump and Mining Museum

Kent St., Iron Mountain
906-774-1086

Exhibits feature regional mineral specimens and various mining equipment, including a 724 ton steeple compound condensing engine.

Iron Mountain Iron Mine

P.O. Box 177, Iron Mountain
906-563-8077 or (off-season) 906-774-7914

Underground tour of the Vulcan mine; ore specimens and mining equipment also on display.

IRONWOOD

Ironwood Area Historical Society Museum

Old Railroad Depot, N. Lowell St.,
P.O. Box 553, Ironwood
906-932-0287

Nostalgic exhibits depicting life on the Gogebic Range, mining memorabilia, and some minerals.

ISHPEMING

Tilden and Empire Mine Tours

Ishpeming to Negaunee Area Chamber of Commerce
661 Palms Ave., Ishpeming
906-486-4841

During the summer months, tours of the open pit iron mines may be arranged through the Chamber of Commerce.

Cliffs Shaft Museum

Marquette Range Iron Mining Heritage Theme Park, Inc.
P.O. Box 555, Ispheming
906-485-1882

Located in the old dry house of the historic Cliffs Shaft mine, this newly created museum features historic photographs, mining memorabilia, and mineral specimens from the Marquette iron range.

KALAMAZOO

Western Michigan University, Department of Geosciences

1187 Rood Hall, Kalamazoo
269-387-5485

Exhibits of minerals, rocks, and fossils.

LAKE LINDEN

Houghton County Historical Museum

5500 Highway M-26, P.O. Box 127, Lake Linden
906-296-4121

Keweenaw mining history and mineral displays.

LANSING

Michigan Historical Museum

717 W. Allegan St., Lansing
517-373-3559

Exhibits featuring copper, iron and industrial minerals mining in Michigan, minerals, and fossils.

Department of Environmental Quality, Geological and Land Management Division

425 W. Allegan St., Lansing
517-241-1515

Displays of Michigan minerals, fossils and rocks.

MARQUETTE

Marquette County Historical Museum

213 North Front Street, Marquette
906-226-3571

Exhibits dealing with the discovery and history of iron mining on the Marquette Range; small display of regional minerals.

MIDLAND

The Hall of Ideas at the Midland Center for the Arts

1801 W. St. Andrews Rd., Midland
989-631-5930 / 24-Hour Event Information Line 800-523-7649
http://www.mcfta.org

A place of discovery where visitors can see, touch, hear and explore Michigan history and geology through three levels of hands-on educational activities. Interactive exhibits feature the geological formation and resources of Michigan, a giant Mastodon skeleton, examination of glacial activity and formation, and fossil exploration. Included are displays with touchable artifacts and exhibitry.

MILFORD

Nature Center for Cultural and Natural History

Kensington Metropolitan Park
2240 West Buno Rd., Milford
248-685-0603

Features temporary and rotating exhibits of various rocks, minerals and fossils.

MOUNT PLEASANT

Musuem of Cultural and Natural History

Central Michigan University
103 Rowe Hall, Bellows and Mission Street, Mount Pleasant
989-774-3829
http://www.museum.cmich.edu/default.htm

Various natural and cultural history exhibits and dioramas, including fossils, rocks and minerals.

MUSKEGON

Muskegon County Museum

430 W. Clay Ave., Muskegon
231-722-0278

Natural history displays, including rocks, minerals, and fossils.

NEGAUNEE

Michigan Iron Industry Museum

73 Forge Rd., Negaunee
906-475-7857
http://www.sos.state.mi.us/history/museum/museiron/

Located on the historic site of the Carp River Forge, the museum's modern exhibits interpret both the industrial and human history of iron mining in Michigan. Some ore specimens are on display. See website for current events and programs.

ONTONAGON

Caledonia Mine

Red Metal Minerals, 109 North Steel Street, Ontonagon
906-884-2488 / copper@red-metal.com

Underground mine tour and mineral collecting by pre-arrangement only.

Ontonagon County Historical Society

422 River St., P.O. Box 92, Ontonagon
906-884-6165

Exhibits featuring native copper and other minerals, Ontonagon boulder replica, and local mining history.

PORT HURON
Port Huron Museum

1115 Sixth St., Port Huron
810-982-0891

Exhibit featuring Michigan minerals and fossils.

ROGERS CITY
Calcite Quarry View

Business-23, 1 mile north of U.S.-23, Rogers City
989-734-2136

Roadside observation viewing area of a limestone operated by Michigan Limestone, Inc.

SAULT STE. MARIE
C. Ernest Kemp Mineral Resources Museum

Lake Superior State University
Crawford Hall, 650 W. Easterday Ave., Sault Ste. Marie
906-632-9537 or 906-635-2267

Expanded exhibits of rocks, minerals, and fossils emphasizing geological processes, Lake Superior geology, and mineral resources are currently under construction.

SOUTH HAVEN
Liberty Hyde Bailey Birth Site Museum

903 S. Bailey Ave., South Haven
269-637-3251

Antiques, Indian artifacts, some minerals.

SOUTH RANGE
Copper Range Historical Society Museum

P.O. Box 148, 44 Trimountain Ave., South Range
906-482-6125

Local mining history and mining memorabilia exhibits.

TRAVERSE CITY
Grand Traverse Heritage Center

322 Sixth St., Traverse City
231-995-0314

Human and natural history exhibits, including the Con Foster collection of minerals and fossils.

WAKEFIELD
Wakefield Historical Society Museum

P.O. Box 1, 306 Sunday Lake St., Wakefield
906-224-8151

Local history displays, including mining; some minerals.

(List provided courtesy of the Michigan Department of Environmental Quality)

Acknowledgments

This book would not have been possible without the help and support of many people. Among those I would like to thank are my parents for their support in my becoming a geologist. Many thanks to John Zawiskie of both the Cranbrook Institute of Science in Bloomfield Hills and the Department of Geology at Wayne State University. John helped cement unconsolidated words and phrases into a cohesive story of Michigan geology. Dr. Troy Holcombe helped explain the exciting lake floor features of the Great Lakes. Thanks to all my professors of geology, and thanks to Peg. Last but not least, many thanks to the director of Wayne State University Press, Jane Hoehner, who by believing in the project from the very beginning made this book a reality.

About the Author

Photograph by P. Mullaly

Charles F. Barker is a geologist with a bachelor's degree in geology from Arizona State University and a master's degree in geology from Boston University. He is a native of Michigan with a lifelong interest in rocks and fossils, and he has been drawing and painting for most of his life. He worked onboard the research vessel *Seamark* mapping the seafloor offshore California, and he currently works in the environmental consulting field, where he investigates sites of groundwater contamination. He is a part-time faculty member of the geology department at Wayne State University and also enjoys teaching children in elementary schools about rocks and fossils.